THIS B
BELON

CW00735030

Name:	Age:

Favourite player:

2019/2020

My Predictions...   **Actual...**

Leeds United's final position:

Leeds United's top scorer:

Championship Winners:

Championship top scorer:

FA Cup Winners:

EFL Cup Winners:

Contributors: Peter Rogers

A TWOCAN PUBLICATION

©2019. Published by twocan under licence from Leeds United Football Club.

Every effort has been made to ensure the accuracy of information within this publication but the publishers cannot be held responsible for any errors or omissions. Views expressed are those of the authors and do not necessarily represent those of the publishers or the football club. All rights reserved.

ISBN: 978-1-911502-75-3

£9

LEEDS UNITED
1919 • 2019
100 YEARS

CONTENTS

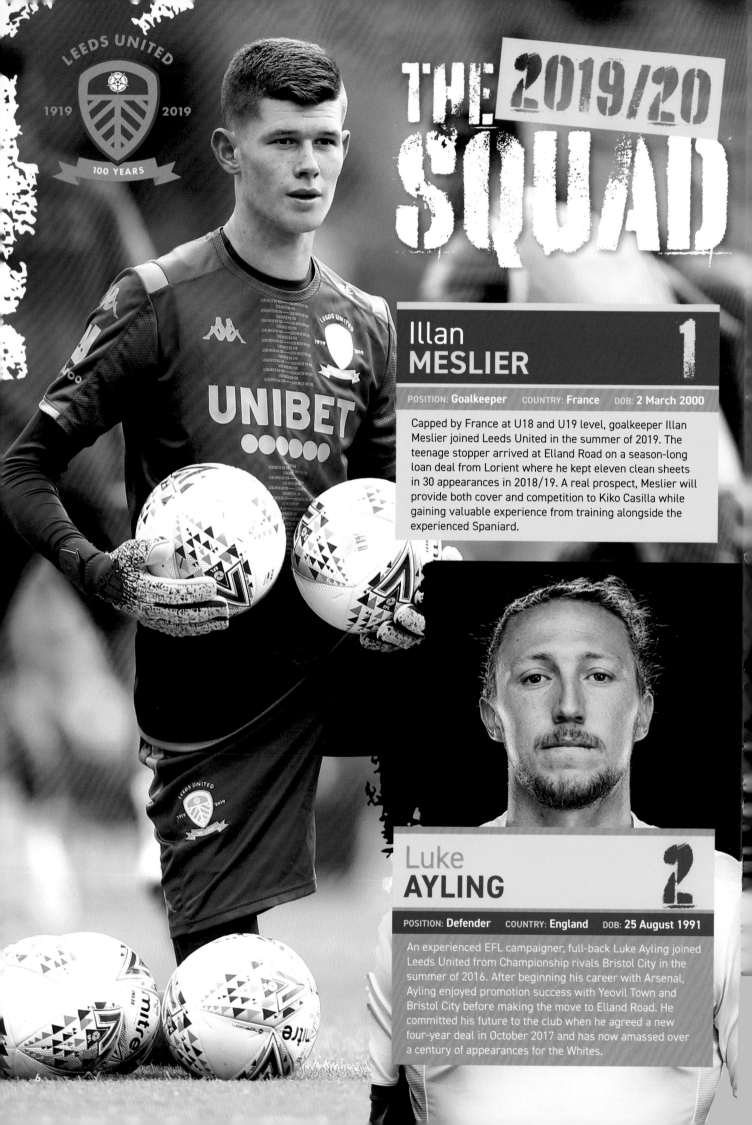

Illan MESLIER 1

POSITION: Goalkeeper   **COUNTRY:** France   **DOB:** 2 March 2000

Capped by France at U18 and U19 level, goalkeeper Illan Meslier joined Leeds United in the summer of 2019. The teenage stopper arrived at Elland Road on a season-long loan deal from Lorient where he kept eleven clean sheets in 30 appearances in 2018/19. A real prospect, Meslier will provide both cover and competition to Kiko Casilla while gaining valuable experience from training alongside the experienced Spaniard.

Luke AYLING 2

POSITION: Defender   **COUNTRY:** England   **DOB:** 25 August 1991

An experienced EFL campaigner, full-back Luke Ayling joined Leeds United from Championship rivals Bristol City in the summer of 2016. After beginning his career with Arsenal, Ayling enjoyed promotion success with Yeovil Town and Bristol City before making the move to Elland Road. He committed his future to the club when he agreed a new four-year deal in October 2017 and has now amassed over a century of appearances for the Whites.

Barry
DOUGLAS
3

POSITION: Defender   **COUNTRY:** Scotland   **DOB:** 4 September 1989

A promotion-winner with Wolves in 2017/18, Barry Douglas signed for Leeds United in July 2018. A much-travelled defender, Douglas stared his career at Queens Park and also played for Dundee United ahead of spells with Lech Poznan and Konyaspor. His first season at Elland Road was cut short by injuries, however the Scot reported back for pre-season in fine form and took his place in Marcelo Bielsa's side for the opening two Championship games of 2019/20.

Adam
FORSHAW
4

POSITION: Midfielder   **COUNTRY:** England   **DOB:** 8 October 1991

Adam Forshaw made the switch from Championship rivals Middlesbrough to Elland Road when he agreed a four-and-a-half year deal with Leeds United in January 2018. The midfielder began his career with Everton before enjoying a promotion-winning spell with Brentford in League One. Stints with Wigan Athletic and Middlesbrough preceded his move to Elland Road and the midfielder will be looking to really make a positive mark on Leeds' 2019/20 Championship campaign.

7

SKILLS: CRUYFF TURN

LEEDS UNITED
1919 · 2019
100 YEARS

1

2 Instead of following through, stop your foot over the ball ...

...and push it back behind your other leg while starting to turn your body.

3

Draw back your foot as if you are going to kick the ball

4 Finish turning through 180° and head in the opposite direction.

5 Your unsuspecting opponent will be left standing wondering what just happened!

Johan Cruyff debuted his signature dummy at the 1974 FIFA World Cup. The trick is a brilliant manoeuvre to fool your opponent and change direction.

LEEDS UNITED
1919 2019
100 YEARS

MATEUSZ KLICH

2018/19

GOAL OF THE SEASON

Leeds United's Goal of the Season award for 2018/19 was won by Polish international midfielder Mateusz Klich for his stunning 25-yard strike in the 1-1 draw at Sheffield Wednesday on Friday 28 September 2018.

Klich was presented with the award at the club's end-of-season awards event in April 2019; on the same evening that Pablo Hernandez was crowned the club's Player of the Season.

In a campaign that saw Leeds hammer home 73 Championship goals, there were certainly plenty of contenders for the award. However, for sheer precision and pace, it was Klich's goal that got the nod.

Ironically, the goal came on an evening when both sides served up memorable strikes for the live Sky television cameras. A keenly-contested Yorkshire derby saw chances come and go at both ends before Wednesday's Adam Reach opened the scoring on the stroke of half-time with a dipping volley from long range.

However, the second half was just nine minutes old when Leeds drew level with a wonder-strike of their own. Attacking the Leppings Lane End where the travelling masses were housed, Klich let fly from all of 25-yards with a driving shot that flew into the top corner of the net leaving Owls' 'keeper Cameron Dawson grasping at thin air.

The goal sparked wild celebrations among the travelling fans as Leeds kept their early season unbeaten away record intact.

Although Klich's Hillsborough howitzer deservedly won him the Goal of the Season award, the midfielder ended an impressive campaign by reaching double figures in the Championship scoring charts.

He also took the mantle of scoring the club's first goal of the 2018/19 season as Leeds United kicked off with an opening weekend victory over Stoke City.

The Pole was then on the scoresheet in the 4-1 demolition of Derby County and hit the net again as Leeds ran out 3-0 winners at Norwich - all inside the opening month of the campaign.

His Goal of the Season against Wednesday will live long in the memory and it was not his only successful trip to South Yorkshire last season - Klich then scored both goals to give Leeds all three points from the trip to Rotherham United in January 2019.

Ben WHITE

5

POSITION: **Defender**   COUNTRY: **England**   DOB: **8 October 1997**

A highly-rated young central-defender, Ben White is on loan from Brighton & Hove Albion for 2019/20. Extremely well thought of by his parent club, White has featured in the Seagulls' first team and has also gained useful experience from previous loan moves. He excelled in League Two with Newport County before stepping up to league One with a loan deal at Peterborough United in the second-half of 2018/19. Comfortable on the ball and swift in the tackle, White looks to bring a real touch of class to the Leeds defence.

Liam COOPER

6

POSITION: **Defender**   COUNTRY: **Scotland**   DOB: **30 August 1991**

A £600,000 signing from Chesterfield in 2014, central defender Liam Cooper has become a tower of strength at the heart of the Whites' defence since arriving at Elland Road. Cooper was appointed club captain by Marcelo Bielsa ahead of the 2018/19 campaign and he skippered the team to the end-of-season Play-Offs. He has now amassed over 150 games in a Leeds shirt and is sure to play another vital role in the 2019/20 season.

Patrick
BAMFORD

9

POSITION: **Striker**   COUNTRY: **England**   DOB: **5 September 1993**

Another player with vast Championship experience, striker Patrick Bamford was Leeds United's star-signing ahead of the 2018/19 season. Bamford joined the Whites from Middlesbrough in July 2018 when he agreed a four-year contract at Elland Road. Despite a number of injuries hampering his first season at the club, plus the goalscoring form of Kemar Roofe, Bamford still managed to contribute nine league goals, including double strikes in the victories over West Bromwich Albion and away to Preston North End.

THE 2019/20 SQUAD

D Wears the Birmingham City captain's armband

 Crystal Palace's nickname **E**

Danish Head Coach at Griffin Park **F**

A Chelsea's Spanish skipper

 The Toffees play their home games here **G**

B Do you recognise this Championship club's crest

H Longest serving Championship manager and a Millwall legend

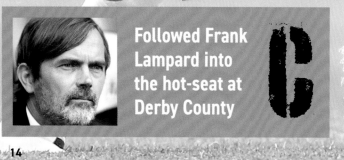 Followed Frank Lampard into the hot-seat at Derby County **C**

I Foxes' Nigeria international signing who wears No.8

LEEDS UNITED
1919 — 2019
100 YEARS

A—Z

2019/20 — PART 1

WHO'S WHO & WHAT'S WHAT OF ENGLISH FOOTBALL?

J Manchester City's Brazilian striker who was part of their 2019 Copa América winning side

K Polish international midfielder who was ever-present for Leeds United last season

This England international has been with the Red Devils since the age of 7

M The Seagulls' Premier League top scorer last season

FAVOURITE...

FOOD? Chocolate

GADGET? PS4

GAME? FIFA

ACTOR? Denzel Washington

PLACE? Vegas

FOOTY FIRSTS...

FIRST PAIR OF FOOTY BOOTS? T90

FIRST BIG INFLUENCE ON YOUR CAREER?
Zinedine Zidane - Baller

FIRST MANAGER YOU PLAYED FOR?
Neil Redfearn

FIRST SPOTTED BY A PRO CLUB? 14

YOUR FIRST GOAL?
Elland Road debut v Cardiff City

QUICKFIRE...

TEA OR COFFEE? Coffee

EARLY BIRD OR NIGHT OWL? Night Owl

ACTION OR COMEDY? Comedy

BATMAN OR SUPERMAN? Batman

CATS OR DOGS? Dogs

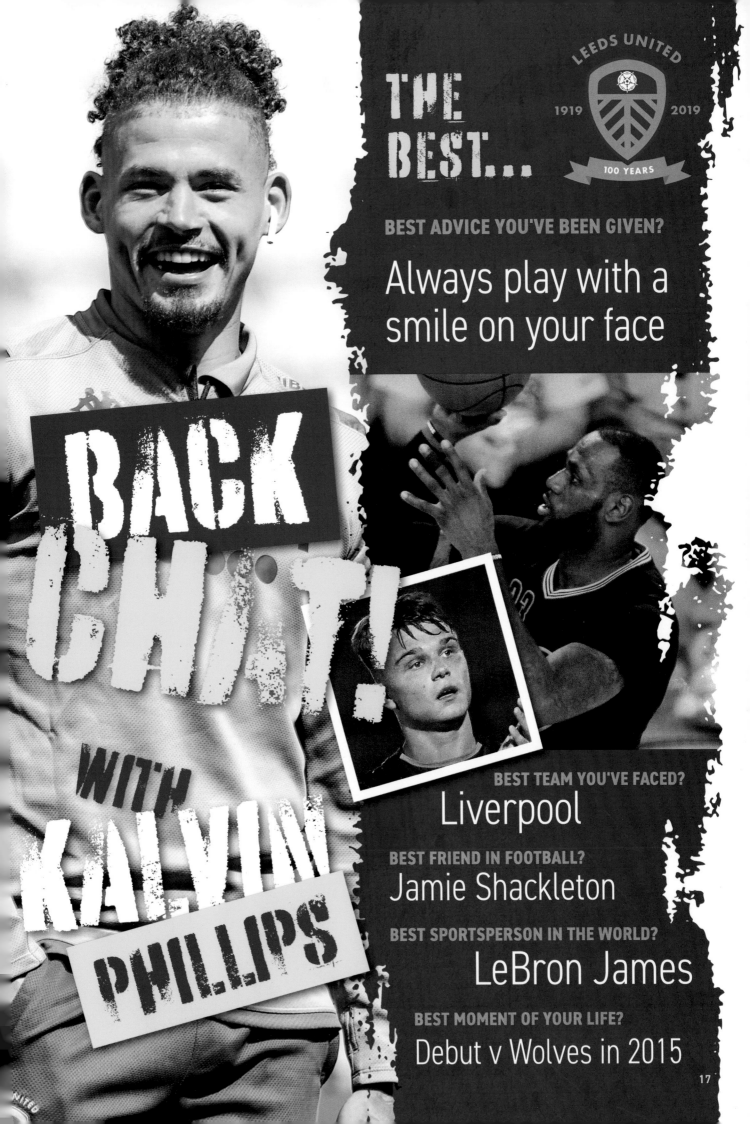

THE BEST...

BEST ADVICE YOU'VE BEEN GIVEN?

Always play with a smile on your face

BACK CHAT!
WITH KALVIN PHILLIPS

BEST TEAM YOU'VE FACED?
Liverpool

BEST FRIEND IN FOOTBALL?
Jamie Shackleton

BEST SPORTSPERSON IN THE WORLD?
LeBron James

BEST MOMENT OF YOUR LIFE?
Debut v Wolves in 2015

17

FACE OFF

Can you figure out who these Leeds stars are?

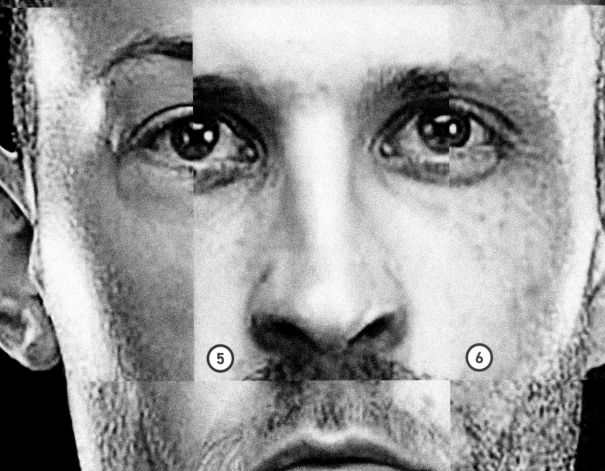

1

2

3

4

5

6

7

8

9

There are five Great Sporting Brits hiding in the crowd... Can you find them?

LEEDS UNITED
1919 — 2019
100 YEARS

Ezgjan
ALIOSKI
10

POSITION: Defender   **COUNTRY:** Macedonia   **DOB:** 12 February 1992

Macedonian international wing-back Ezgjan Aliosko proved to be one of the first names on Marcelo Bielsa's Leeds United teamsheet in 2018/19, as the Whites battled with Norwich City and Sheffield United for automatic promotion. Alioski scored seven Championship goals last season including a vital second-half winner at home to Bolton Wanderers in February 2019. He originally joined the Whites in the summer of 2017 from Swiss side Lugano.

THE 2019/20 SQUAD

Tyler
ROBERTS
11

POSITION: Striker   **COUNTRY:** Wales   **DOB:** 12 January 1999

Young striker Tyler Roberts has already sampled Premier League action with West Bromwich Albion and full international football with Wales. He began his career at the Hawthorns and took in beneficial loan spells with Oxford United, Shrewsbury Town and Walsall before agreeing to a switch to Elland Road during the 2018 January transfer window. An impressive performer for Leeds in 2018/19, Roberts rivalled Jack Clarke for the club's Young Player of the Year award.

Kiko
CASILLA

13

POSITION: **Goalkeeper**   COUNTRY: **Spain**   DOB: **2 October 1986**

Leeds United pulled off something of a transfer sensation when goalkeeper Kiko Casilla was signed from Spanish giants Real Madrid during the 2019 January transfer window. The vastly-experienced 'keeper, who was part of three Champions League-winning sides with Real, agreed a four-and-a-half year deal at Elland Road. He made his debut in a 2-1 win away to Yorkshire rivals Rotherham United and his presence adds real confidence to those playing in front of him.

Eddie
NKETIAH

14

POSITION: **Striker**   COUNTRY: **England**   DOB: **30 May 1999**

On loan from Premier League Arsenal for the 2019/20 season, the arrival of striker Eddie Nketiah at Leeds United in August 2019 certainly sparked a level of excitement around Elland Road. He has eight Premier League appearances and one goal to his name with Arsenal. A product of the Gunners' Academy, Nketiah burst on to the scene with a brace on his home debut for Arsenal as they defeated Norwich City in the League Cup in October 2017.

FAVOURITE...

FOOD? Pizza

GADGET? Phone

GAME? Fortnite

ACTOR? Kevin Hart

PLACE? New York

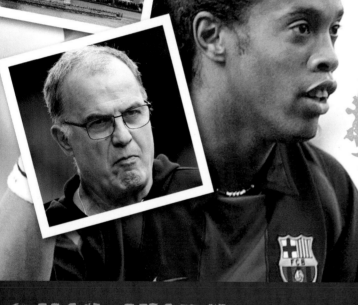

FOOTY FIRSTS...

FIRST PAIR OF BOOTS? Predators

FIRST BIG INFLUENCE ON YOUR CAREER? Ronaldinho - Just Class

FIRST MANAGER YOU PLAYED FOR? Marcelo Bielsa

FIRST SPOTTED BY A PRO CLUB? 6

YOUR FIRST GOAL? Scoring five v Manchester United

QUICKFIRE...

TEA OR COFFEE? Coffee

EARLY BIRD OR NIGHT OWL? Night Owl

ACTION OR COMEDY? Comedy

BATMAN OR SUPERMAN? Superman

CATS OR DOGS? Dogs

THE BEST...

BEST ADVICE YOU'VE BEEN GIVEN?

Play with freedom

BACK CHAT! WITH JACK CLARKE

BEST TEAM YOU'VE FACED?
Norwich City

BEST FRIEND IN FOOTBALL?
Kalvin Phillips

BEST SPORTSPERSON IN THE WORLD?
Cristiano Ronaldo

BEST MOMENT OF YOUR LIFE?
Debut v Brentford in 2018

PATRICK BAMFORD

9

Colour in
this picture of
Patrick Bamford

PATRICK
BAMFORD

Helder
COSTA
17

POSITION: Midfielder   **COUNTRY:** Portugal   **DOB:** 12 January 1994

Leeds United's standout summer signing ahead of the 2019/20 campaign, Portuguese winger Helder Costa arrived at Elland Road on a season-long loan deal from Wolverhampton Wanderers. A tricky wide-man who is blessed with phenomenal pace, Costa was a star performer for Wolves in their 2017/18 Championship promotion-winning campaign and helped the Molineux club to a seventh-place finish in the Premier League last season.

Stuart
DALLAS
15

POSITION: Defender   **COUNTRY:** Northern Ireland   **DOB:** 19 April 1991

Northern Ireland international defender Stuart Dallas has made over 150 appearances for Leeds United after joining the club from Brentford in the summer of 2015. The defender was a 2014 League One promotion-winner in a Brentford side that included current Leeds teammate Adam Forshaw. His first season at Elland Road saw the Irishman voted the Players' Player of the Season for 2015/16.

Pablo
HERNANDEZ
19

POSITION: Midfielder   **COUNTRY:** Spain   **DOB:** 11 April 1985

Very much the main man in the Leeds United midfield, Pablo Hernandez was voted the Whites' Player of the Season for 2018/19. The highly-talented Spaniard has now won the award on a back-to-back basis having also landed the honour in 2017/18. Hernandez scored 12 goals for Leeds in 2018/19 and the attacking midfielder was among the goals early in the 2019/20 campaign netting in both of the Whites' first two Championship fixtures.

Jack
HARRISON
22

POSITION: Midfielder   **COUNTRY:** England   **DOB:** 20 November 1996

England U21 international Jack Harrison impressed throughout the 2018/19 season while on loan at Elland Road from Premier League champions Manchester City. The summer of 2019 saw Harrison agree a second loan deal at Elland Road and the midfielder marked his second debut for Leeds United with the third goal in the Whites' opening-day 3-1 win away to Bristol City.

THE 2019/20
SQUAD

29

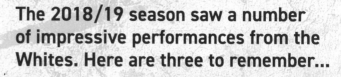

REWIND

LEEDS UNITED 3
BLACKBURN ROVERS 2

Leeds United produced a sensational finish at Elland Road, scoring twice in time added on, to register an incredible 3-2 Boxing Day Championship victory over Blackburn Rovers.

The hosts had taken a first-half lead when Rovers' defender Derrick Williams sliced Jack Harrison's cross into his own net. Blackburn drew level two minutes into the second half with a Charlie Mulgrew penalty and honours looked like ending even until Mulgrew netted his and Rovers' second goal of the game in the final minute. However, Leeds managed to snatch victory from the jaws of defeat. Firstly Kemar Roofe scrambled home an injury-time equaliser before then sending the home fans into raptures when he headed in a 94th-minute winner.

LEEDS UNITED 4
WEST BROMWICH ALBION 0

Marcelo Bielsa's team really turned on the style to thrash fellow promotion-chasers West Bromwich Albion 4-0 at Elland Road on Friday 1 March 2019.

The home fans among a crowd of 35,888 were soon up and out of their seats after Pablo Hernandez opened the scoring after just 16 seconds. Patrick Bamford extended Leeds' advantage with a second goal after 28 minutes.

The home side continued to dominate after the beak and Bamford grabbed his second and Leeds' third goal of the night after 63 minutes. Ezgjan Alioski completed the rout with the fourth goal of the game two minutes into time added on.

PRESTON NORTH END 0
LEEDS UNITED 2

After a surprise 1-0 defeat at Birmingham City four days earlier, Leeds United returned to winning ways with an impressive performance away to Preston North End on 9 April 2019.

In front of a large travelling contingent, Patrick Bamford unleashed a thunderous 25-yard shot to break the deadlock shortly after the hour-mark.

Bamford then headed home his and Leeds' second goal of the game to seal all three points with 14 minutes left to play. This vital win saw Leeds back in the automatic promotion places as the three-way battle for promotion with Norwich City and Sheffield United entered its final month.

Answer these questions on the 2018/19 campaign and see how much attention you were paying LAST SEASON!

1. Who made the most League appearances for Leeds last season (excluding Play-Offs)?

ANSWER

2. Who netted Leeds United's first Championship goal last season?

ANSWER

3. How many points did Leeds United finish the 2018/19 season with?

ANSWER

4. How many League goals did the Whites score last season (excluding Play-Offs)?

ANSWER

5. What was the highest home attendance of 2018/19?

ANSWER

6. Against which two clubs did the Whites hit four league goals (excluding Play-Offs)?

ANSWER

7. Who scored the winning goal in the EFL Cup win over Bolton Wanderers?

ANSWER

8. Who knocked Leeds United out of the FA Cup in the third round?

ANSWER

9. Who received the most yellow cards in the league last season?

ANSWER

10. Name the two players who received a red card during the league during 2018/19?

ANSWER

11. Who did the Whites sign from Real Madrid during the January transfer window?

ANSWER

12. Who top-scored for the Whites in the Championship last season?

ANSWER

ANSWERS ON PAGE 62

FAST FORWARD

There are lots of exciting games ahead for the Whites in the second half of the 2019/20 Championship campaign.

Here are three potential crackers...

SHEFFIELD WEDNESDAY (H)
11 January 2020

Leeds United's first home game of the calendar year of 2020 sees Sheffield Wednesday provide the opposition for what is sure to be an eagerly-anticipated Yorkshire derby.

Last season saw a 1-1 draw at Hillsborough before the two sides met at Elland Road in the closing weeks of the 2018/19 campaign. Leeds came out on top 1-0 in the home fixture when a 65th minute goal from Jack Harrison settled a hard-fought match in their favour.

With 39 wins, 25 draws and 33 defeats against the Owls, Leeds will be looking to extend their head-to-head superiority over their Yorkshire rivals in 2019/20.

FULHAM (H)
18 March 2020

Relegated from the Premier League at the end of last season, big-spending Fulham are widely expected to be serious promotion challengers in 2019/20.

The Cottagers match at Elland Road in March 2020 certainly looks set to be one of Leeds' toughest and challenging assignments of the season.

Under the management of Scott Parker, the Londoners have maintained the services many star players, including Serbian striker Aleksandar Mitrovic. They have also added Brighton & Hove Albion front-man Anthony Knockaert to their ranks in their bid for an immediate return to the top flight. Leeds United v Fulham certainly appears a standout fixture in 2019/20 Championship calendar.

DERBY COUNTY (A)
25 April 2020

After doubling the Rams in the regulation 2018/19 Championship season, before meeting in the Play-Off semi-finals, Leeds United and Derby County will lock horns once again in 2019/20.

The Rams are now under the management of former Dutch international Phillip Cocu following Frank Lampard's brief stint in charge. Elland Road will provide the venue for the first meeting of the season between these two rivals on 21 September 2019.

However, the second clash of the season at Pride Park in April 2020 is Leeds' final away game of the season and could well be an intriguing affair as the campaign reaches its climax.

PREMIER LEAGUE

OUR PREDICTION FOR PREMIER LEAGUE WINNERS:

MANCHESTER CITY

YOUR PREDICTION:

OUR PREDICTION FOR PREMIER LEAGUE RUNNERS-UP:

LIVERPOOL

YOUR PREDICTION:

CHAMPIONSHIP

OUR PREDICTION FOR CHAMPIONSHIP WINNERS:

LEEDS UNITED

YOUR PREDICTION:

OUR PREDICTION FOR CHAMPIONSHIP RUNNERS-UP:

DERBY COUNTY

YOUR PREDICTION:

THE FA CUP

OUR PREDICTION FOR FA CUP WINNERS:

ARSENAL

YOUR PREDICTION:

OUR PREDICTION FOR FA CUP RUNNERS-UP:

EVERTON

YOUR PREDICTION:

EFL CUP

OUR PREDICTION FOR EFL CUP WINNERS:

LEICESTER CITY

YOUR PREDICTION:

OUR PREDICTION FOR EFL CUP RUNNERS-UP:

WATFORD

YOUR PREDICTION:

2020 PREDICTIONS

TEAM WORK

Every Championship team is hidden in the grid, except one!
Can you figure out which is missing?

Barnsley

Birmingham City

Blackburn Rovers

Brentford

Bristol City

Cardiff City

Charlton Athletic

Derby County

Fulham

Huddersfield Town

Hull City

Leeds United

Luton Town

Middlesbrough

Millwall

Nottingham Forest

Preston North End

Queens Park Rangers

Reading

Sheffield Wednesday

Stoke City

Swansea City

West Bromwich Albion

Wigan Athletic

```
A R D N E H T R O N N O T S E R P
D A O V Y U O B S C S A W U T V B
W Y T I C L O T S I R B F E V R N
A V U E R L E Q V P E Y I L C O U
I R M O W C Y U G D E N D A T L L
A P A B J I Z E J L U B H S L G U
T L H I C T X E S A T Y O A S Q T
Q C L G F Y E N V T S F W J K P O
P H U D D E R S F I E L D T O W N
I A F H M A S P V T L N R W X E T
W R D S B M I A O I F U C M Z S O
T L Y K H N E R M Y J Y A I R T W
A T S C A H S K G K L T R K T B N
P O A W R I V R J G N I D A E R R
H N I T A U C A K X U C I E V O L
N A O S O N H N W O L E F W H M P
J T S E B S S G T J C K F J G W N
P H M R N G B E V R V O C Q U I Y
C L V O E B G R A H G T I L O C T
A E B F K V P S E C A S T D R H I
Z T O M S G O E O N I B Y T B A C
V I F A E S F R B U T T E K S L M
O C W H O Q L B N R S F Y N E B A
F U C G B I T Q A R Y X O E L I H
O N H N R A M N W T U M I R D O G
U J A I Y T N U O C Y B R E D N
N P D T L C V C P I D Z K P I B
I E G T M S A O D J M F U C M P M
Y N K O X N D H A B O M A S A F R
E D T N O D E T I N U S D E E L I
W I G A N A T H L E T I C B T R B
```

ANSWERS ON PAGE 62

LEEDS UNITED
1919 2019
100 YEARS

32Red

COOPER
6

Ex-Hammer who made his debut for the Golden Boys last season

 **Middlesbrough keeper who played all 46 league games last season**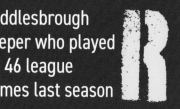

Joint Premier League top scorer last season alongside teammate Mané and Arsenal's Aubameyang

France international who joined Spurs from Olympique Lyonnais in July 2019

 **Nickname of Yorkshire club Barnsley**

Goalkeeper and local lad who came through the ranks at Norwich

 **The Rams' team kit manufacturer**

 **Former England international in the manager's seat at Craven Cottage**

 **The home of Championship new boys Charlton Athletic**

36

W Managed the Blades to promotion to the Premier League

X Switzerland international who plays his home games at the Emirates Stadium

LEEDS UNITED
1919   2019
100 YEARS

A–Z 2019/20 PART 2

WHO'S WHO & WHAT'S WHAT OF ENGLISH FOOTBALL?

Y The Magpies' international right-back with over 50 USA caps

Z Hammers defender capped over 50 times by Argentina

THE 2019/20 SQUAD

Kalvin PHILLIPS — 23

POSITION: Midfielder   **COUNTRY:** England   **DOB:** 2 December 1995

Homegrown hero Kalvin Phillips has progressed through the youth and reserve ranks at Thorp Arch to make over 125 appearances for Leeds United. He initially broke into the first team in 2015 and his committed all-action displays have won him many admirers. The 2018/19 season saw Phillips' name entered into the Leeds United record books when he netted an equaliser away to Middlesbrough in the 101st minute of the match - this was timed as the club's latest-ever goal in a league fixture.

Gaetano BERARDI — 28

POSITION: Defender   **COUNTRY:** Switzerland   **DOB:** 21 August 1988

Gaetano Berardi is a versatile defender who can operate in either full-back berth or in a central-defensive role if called upon. A Swiss international, Berardi joined Leeds back in 2014 from Italian giants Sampdoria. Injury saw him miss a large chunk of the 2018/19 campaign and he will be looking to regain both full fitness and his place in the side for the 2019/20 season.

Alfie McCALMONT 38

POSITION: **Midfielder**   COUNTRY: **Northern Ireland**   DOB: **25 March 2000**

2019 proved a great success for teenage midfielder Alfie McCalmont. The Thirsk-born defensive-midfielder agreed a new professional contract in January and after continuing to impress in the club's U23 side, he stepped up to the first-team scene in August. After making his debut in the League Cup first round tie with Salford as a 70th minute substitute, he then made his full debut starting the second round match with Stoke City at Elland Road. Already capped by Northern Ireland at U21 level, McCalmont is certainly one to watch in 2019/20.

Leif DAVIS 40

POSITION: **Defender**   COUNTRY: **England**   DOB: **31 December 1999**

Young defender Leif Davis was recruited from League Two Morecambe in the summer of 2018 and made his Leeds United debut in the thrilling 3-2 victory away to Aston Villa in December 2018. Something of a lucky charm for Leeds United, he featured in four Championship fixtures in 2018/19 and the Whites won them all! His first appearance of the 2018/19 season saw him come off of the bench in the 3-1 opening-day triumph at Ashton Gate.

Mateusz KLICH 43

POSITION: **Midfielder**   COUNTRY: **Poland**   DOB: **13 January 1990**

Mateusz Klich made a flying start to his 2018/19 season with two goals in the opening games of the season as the Whites registered comprehensive wins over Stoke City and Derby County. Klich joined the club in 2017 from Dutch side FC Twente and after spending a loan spell with FC Utrecht in the second half of the 2017/18 campaign, he made his mark on the first-team scene at Elland Road last season and also netted the club's Goal of the Season in the 1-1 draw away to Sheffield Wednesday.

LEEDS UNITED
ELLAND ROAD
CAPACITY: 37,890

HUDDERSFIELD TOWN
THE JOHN SMITH'S STADIUM
CAPACITY: 24,500

BLACKBURN ROVERS
EWOOD PARK
CAPACITY: 31,367

PRESTON NORTH END
DEEPDALE
CAPACITY: 23,404

WIGAN ATHLETIC
DW STADIUM
CAPACITY: 25,133

BARNSLEY
OAKWELL
CAPACITY: 23,287

STOKE CITY
BET365 STADIUM
CAPACITY: 30,022

WEST BROMWICH ALBION
THE HAWTHORNS
CAPACITY: 26,850

BIRMINGHAM CITY
ST ANDREW'S
CAPACITY: 29,409

SWANSEA CITY
LIBERTY STADIUM
CAPACITY: 21,088

BRENTFORD
GRIFFIN PARK
CAPACITY: 12,763

CARDIFF CITY
CARDIFF CITY STADIUM
CAPACITY: 33,280

BRISTOL CITY
ASHTON GATE
CAPACITY: 27,000

READING
MADEJSKI STADIUM
CAPACITY: 24,161

MIDDLESBROUGH
RIVERSIDE STADIUM
CAPACITY: 34,742

HULL CITY
KCOM STADIUM
CAPACITY: 25,586

LEEDS UNITED
1919 — 2019
100 YEARS

CHAMPIONSHIP GROUNDS 2019/20

SHEFFIELD WEDNESDAY
HILLSBOROUGH STADIUM
CAPACITY: 39,732

Take a look at where Leeds will be heading this season to take on their rivals.

Tick the grounds off once we've visited!

NOTTINGHAM FOREST
CITY GROUND
CAPACITY: 30,445

DERBY COUNTY
PRIDE PARK STADIUM
CAPACITY: 33,597

LUTON TOWN
KENILWORTH ROAD
CAPACITY: 10,356

QUEENS PARK RANGERS
KIYAN PRINCE FOUNDATION STADIUM
CAPACITY: 18,439

CHARLTON ATHLETIC
THE VALLEY
CAPACITY: 27,111

MILLWALL
THE DEN
CAPACITY: 20,146

FULHAM
CRAVEN COTTAGE
CAPACITY: 25,700

SKILLS: RAINBOW KICK

LEEDS UNITED
1919   2019
100 YEARS

1
Start off with your feet on either side of the ball

2
Use one foot to roll the ball up your other leg

3
Make sure to roll the ball hard enough to give it some air

4
When the ball is in the air strike it with your heel

5
...and flick it over your head!

Brazilian star striker, Neymar, is well known for his use of the rainbow kick on the pitch and regularly fools his opposition. The trick is an impressive show of skill which takes practise, practise practise!

TIP: Lean forward as you're doing the trick, this helps create space between you and the ball so you can strike it more easily.

43

HEY REF!

Do you always know what the officials are signalling?

Take a look at these and see if you are up to the job...

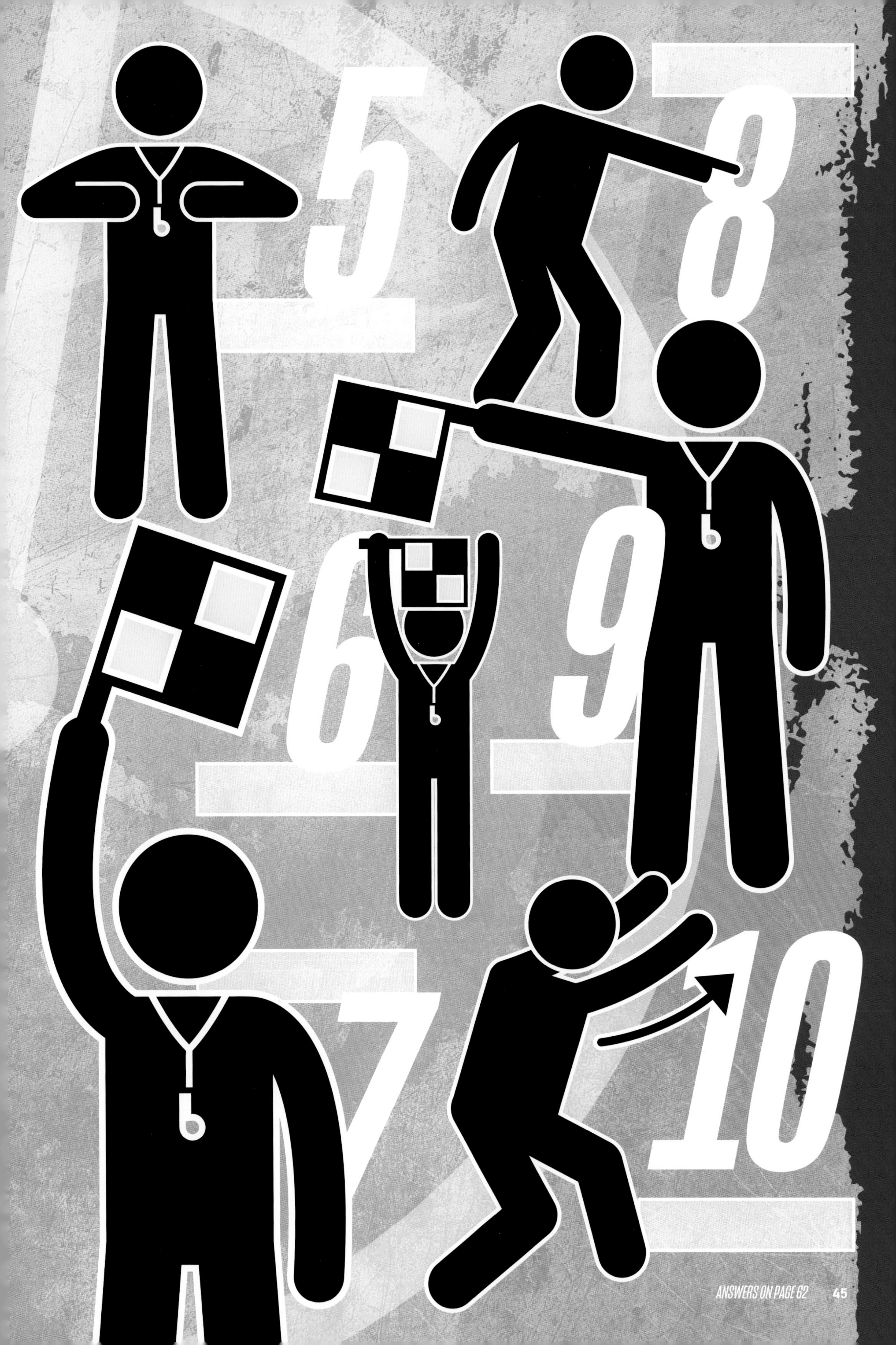

ANSWERS ON PAGE 62

FAVOURITE...

FOOD? Chicken Nuggets

GADGET? Phone

GAME? FIFA

ACTOR? Leonardo DiCaprio

PLACE? Zante

FOOTY FIRSTS...

FIRST PAIR OF BOOTS? Predators

FIRST BIG INFLUENCE ON YOUR CAREER?
Fernando Torres - Banged them in

FIRST MANAGER YOU PLAYED FOR?
Marcelo Bielsa

FIRST SPOTTED BY A PRO CLUB? 6

YOUR FIRST LEAGUE GAME?
2-2 at Swansea City, 21 August 2018

QUICKFIRE...

TEA OR COFFEE? Tea

EARLY BIRD OR NIGHT OWL? Early Bird

ACTION OR COMEDY? Comedy

BATMAN OR SUPERMAN? Batman

CATS OR DOGS? Dogs

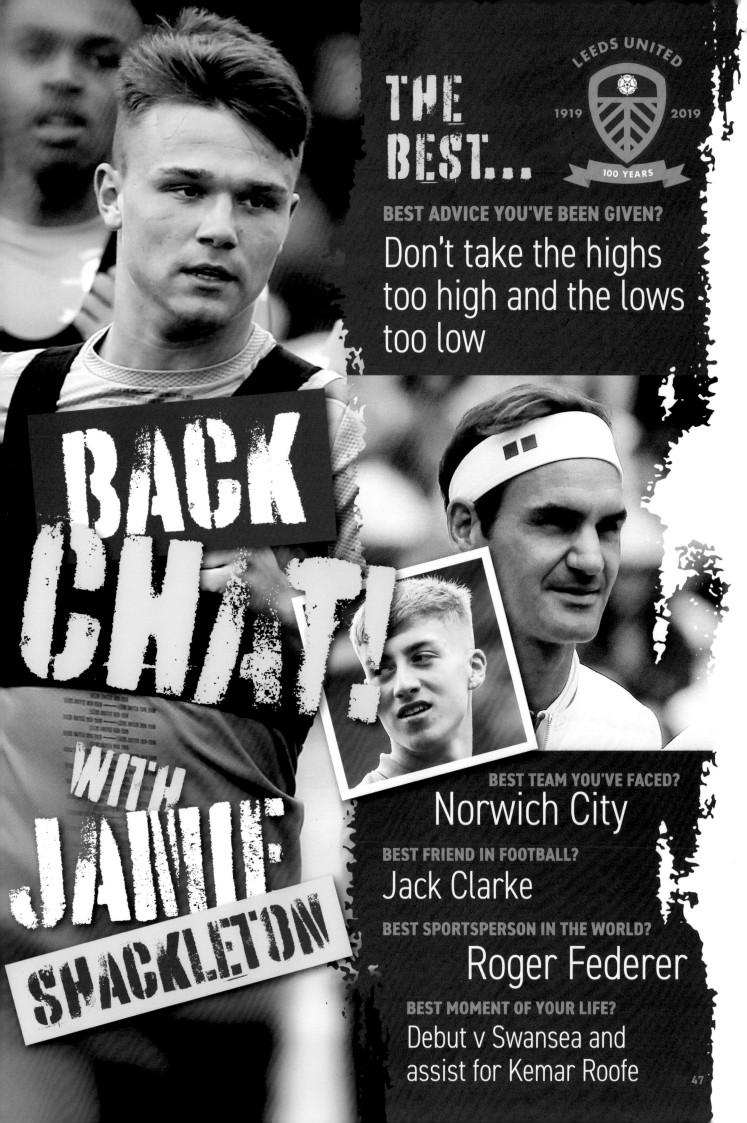

THE BEST...

LEEDS UNITED
1919 · 2019
100 YEARS

BEST ADVICE YOU'VE BEEN GIVEN?
Don't take the highs too high and the lows too low

BACK CHAT!
WITH JAMIE SHACKLETON

BEST TEAM YOU'VE FACED?
Norwich City

BEST FRIEND IN FOOTBALL?
Jack Clarke

BEST SPORTSPERSON IN THE WORLD?
Roger Federer

BEST MOMENT OF YOUR LIFE?
Debut v Swansea and assist for Kemar Roofe

47

SKILLS: MARADONA SPIN

1
Start off by simply dribbling the ball

2
While moving in a forward motion, tap the ball with your leading foot...

3
...and start turning your body in the opposite direction

4
As you're spinning, pull the ball back with your other foot while continuing to turn

5

6
Then keep moving forward!

Argentinian maestro, Maradona, is very well known for this move. It is brilliant for overcoming opponents and getting yourself into space, as while you are spinning you are putting your back to the defender and shielding the ball.

THE CHAMPIONSHIP 2019/20

BARNSLEY

BIRMINGHAM CITY

BLACKBURN ROVERS

BRENTFORD

BRISTOL CITY

CARDIFF CITY

CHARLTON ATHLETIC

DERBY COUNTY

FULHAM

HUDDERSFIELD TOWN

HULL CITY

LEEDS UNITED

Get to know Leeds United's rivals in full Championship colour!

LUTON TOWN

MIDDLESBROUGH

MILLWALL

NOTTINGHAM FOREST

PRESTON NORTH END

QUEENS PARK RANGERS

READING

SHEFFIELD WEDNESDAY

STOKE CITY

SWANSEA CITY

WEST BROMWICH ALBION

WIGAN ATHLETIC

PABLO
HERNANDEZ

2018/19

PLAYER OF THE SEASON

Spanish international midfielder Pablo Hernandez collected the club's Player of the Season award following a series of outstanding performances during the 2018/19 campaign.

The award saw Hernandez confirmed as the club's top performer for the second campaign running, having also been named Player of the Season in 2017/18. The former Spain international picked up the award at a ceremony at Elland Road at the end of April with the 2018/19 season widely being acknowledged as his finest campaign since joining the club in 2016.

The popular midfield maestro received both the club's Player of the Season award and the Players' Player of the Season award, having served up twelve goals and twelve assists as Leeds landed an end-of-season Championship Play-Off place.

Hernandez was in sparkling form throughout the season and set the tone for a positive campaign when he netted in the opening-day victory over Stoke City. The driving force behind the side's flying start to the season, the Spaniard was also on target against Swansea City and Norwich City as Leeds marched to the top of the Championship table.

After notching three further Championship goals in November, Hernandez carried his scoring form into December grabbing the only goal of the game to seal all three points away to promotion rivals Sheffield United.

A memorable brace in the thrilling 3-2 Elland Road victory over Millwall in March proved to be his final goals from a season that saw him make a total of 41 appearances for the club.

One of the first names on boss Marcelo Bielsa's teamsheet, Hernandez scored the club's opening goal of the 2019/20 campaign with a stunning strike away to Bristol City. Only time will tell as to if he can make it a hat-trick of Player of the Season awards in 2019/20? One thing is for sure, not many at Elland Road would bet against it!

YOUNG PLAYER OF THE SEASON

Teenage winger Jack Clarke enjoyed a breakthrough season in 2018/19 and ended the campaign as the club's Young Player of the Season.

Clarke made his senior debut in October 2018 and went on to make 25 first-team appearances, netting his first goal for the club in the 3-2 win away at Aston Villa.

Such was the teenager's progress in 2018/19 that he sealed a multi-million pound move to Champions League finalists Tottenham Hotspur in the summer of 2019. Part of the deal was that Clarke returned to Elland Road on a season-long loan for 2019/20.

Mateusz BOGUSZ 44

POSITION: **Midfielder**   COUNTRY: **Poland**   DOB: **22 August 2001**

Attacking-midfielder Matesuz was recruited from Ruch Chorzow in January 2019. The Polish U20 international agreed a two-and-a-half year deal at Elland Road and soon worked his way into the first-team squad. He was an unused substitute on several occasions at the end of 2018/19 and after impressing in pre-season, Bogusz was handed a taste of first-team action when he started the League Cup second round match with Stoke City at Elland Road.

Jamie SHACKLETON 46

POSITION: **Midfielder**   COUNTRY: **England**   DOB: **8 October 1999**

Midfielder Jamie Shackleton has progressed from the Leeds United Academy to play first-team football for his boyhood club. An impressive pre-season was rewarded with a first-team debut in August 2018 when he replaced Mateusz Klich during the second half of the Whites' 4-1 win at Derby County. After a first start in the League Cup victory over Bolton Wanderers, Shackleton went on to feature in 24 first-team matches in 2018/19.

Jack CLARKE

47

POSITION: **Midfielder**   COUNTRY: **England**   DOB: **23 November 2000**

Young Player of the Season at Elland Road in 2018/19, Jack Clarke made 25 first-team appearances for Leeds United in what was his breakthrough campaign. The talented youngster netted his first senior goal in the 3-2 win over Aston Villa in December 2018 and his performances won him rave reviews. Such was his form last season that he earned a big-money move to Tottenham Hotspur in the summer of 2019. His move to Spurs was agreed with an immediate loan move back to Elland Road for 2019/20.

Jordan STEVENS

48

POSITION: **Midfielder**   COUNTRY: **England**   DOB: **25 March 2000**

Signed from Forest Green Rovers in February 2018, Jordan Stevens is a midfield player blessed with great close control and pace. With the ability to operate either centrally or in a wide role, Stevens made his first-team debut in the Whites' Championship match away to Stoke City in January 2019. The youngster will clearly be looking to continue his development during the 2019/20 campaign.

THE 2019/20 SQUAD

KALVIN PHILLIPS
23

56

Elland Road

Leeds   LS11

LEEDS UNITED
1919   2019
100 YEARS

COVER THE WALL IN POSTERS!

Leeds United have boasted a wealth of talent over the years! Here is our...

WHITES DREAM TEAM

...see if you agree!

GOALKEEPER

LUKIC
1

JOHN LUKIC

Goalkeeper John Lukic was ever-present in the club's 1991/92 Championship title-winning season. A former England U21 international, Lukic had two spells at Elland Road with a stint at Arsenal sandwiched in between.

YOUR CHOICE

DEFENDER

REANEY
2

PAUL REANEY

England international right-back Paul Reaney enjoyed a trophy-laden career with Leeds United. A Second Division title winner in 1963/64 and a First Division champion in both 1968/69 and 1973/74, Reaney was also an FA Cup winner with Leeds in 1971/72.

YOUR CHOICE

DEFENDER

HUNTER
6

NORMAN HUNTER

Tough-tackling England international central-defender, Norman Hunter began his career at Elland Road and was a Second Division title winner in 1963/64. A League Cup winner in 1967/68, Hunter was twice a First Division champion and an FA Cup winner in 1972.

YOUR CHOICE

MIDFIELDER

LORIMER
7

PETER LORIMER

A Scotland international, Peter Lorimer holds the record as Leeds United's record league goalscorer having netted 168 goals in 525 league games for the club. He was the club's youngest player when he made his debut aged 15 years and 289 days old against Southampton in September 1962 and went on to help the club to a host of honours.

YOUR CHOICE

FORWARD

CLARKE
8

ALLAN CLARKE

Famed for heading home Leeds United's winner in the 1972 FA Cup Final, Allan Clarke set a new British transfer record when he sealed a £160,000 move from Leicester City in July 1968. Clarke netted an impressive 110 league goals Leeds in 273 games for the club.

YOUR CHOICE

DEFENDER

COOPER 3

TERRY COOPER

Left-back Terry Cooper netted Leeds United's winning goal in the 1968 League Cup Final triumph and was capped by England while at Elland Road. Cooper made 250 league appearances for Leeds and netted seven goals for the Whites.

YOUR CHOICE

MIDFIELDER

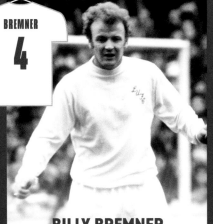

BREMNER 4

BILLY BREMNER

Leeds United's inspirational captain during the successful Don Revie era at Elland Road. Bremner played in a colossal 586 league games for the club, scoring 90 goals. He also starred in two Fairs Cup final triumphs and was a European Cup and European Cup Winners' Cup finalist.

YOUR CHOICE

DEFENDER

CHARLTON 5

JACK CHARLTON

A World Cup-winner with England in 1966, central-defender Jack Charlton was capped 35 times while with Leeds United. A league champion and an FA Cup winner, Charlton made 629 league appearances for Leeds and was voted Footballer of the Year in 1967.

YOUR CHOICE

FORWARD

CHARLES 9

JOHN CHARLES

Legendary Welsh international, John Charles enjoyed two successful spells with Leeds United. He was leading scorer in Leeds' 1955/56 promotion success after netting a club record 42 goals in a season during 1953/54. Charles joined Italian giants Juventus in May 1957 for a world record £65,000 before returning to Elland Road in the summer of 1962.

YOUR CHOICE

MIDFIELDER

GILES 10

JOHNNY GILES

Johnny Giles joined Leeds United from Manchester United in 1963 and was the creative spark in Don Revie's team that enjoyed success both domestically and in Europe. A Republic of Ireland international, Giles scored 88 goals in 383 league games while at Elland Road.

YOUR CHOICE

MIDFIELDER

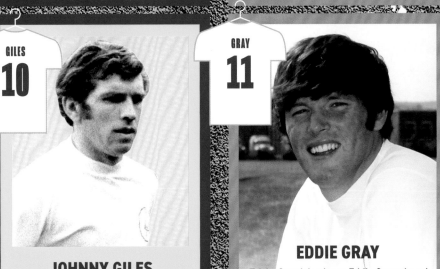

GRAY 11

EDDIE GRAY

Tricky Scottish winger Eddie Gray played a vital role in Leeds' League Cup and Fairs Cup successes in 1967/68, before enjoying First Division title success the following season. Gray was also an FA Cup winner with the Whites in 1972 in a career that saw him play 455 league games for Leeds United.

YOUR CHOICE

TOP 10

MY TOP 10...

MOMENTS OF THIS YEAR

1.
2.
3.
4.
5.
6.
7.
8.
9.
10.

MY TOP 10...

FOOTBALLERS OF ALL TIME

1.
2.
3.
4.
5.
6.
7.
8.
9.
10.

MY TOP 10...

LEEDS UNITED MEMORIES

1.
2.
3.
4.
5.
6.
7.
8.
9.
10.

MY TOP 10...

RESOLUTIONS FOR 2020

1.
2.
3.
4.
5.
6.
7.
8.
9.
10.

BEN WHITE

5

LEEDS UNITED
1919 • 2019
100 YEARS

QUIZ ANSWERS

PAGE 14 · A-Z PART ONE

A. César Azpilicueta. B. Bristol City.
C. Phillip Cocu. D. Harlee Dean. E. The Eagles.
F. Thomas Frank, Brentford. G. Goodison Park.
H. Neil Harris. I. Kelechi Iheanacho. J. Gabriel Jesus.
K. Mateusz Klich. L. Jesse Lingard. M. Glenn Murray.

PAGE 19 · FACE OFF

1. Kalvin Phillips. 2. Ezgjan Alioski. 3. Luke Ayling.
4. Ben White. 5. Mateusz Klich. 6. Adam Forshaw.
7. Pablo Hernandez. 8. Liam Cooper. 9. Kiko Casilla.

PAGE 20 · FAN'TASTIC

Owen Farrell, Lewis Hamilton Johanna Konta,
Anthony Joshua and Ben Stokes.

PAGE 31 · REWIND

1. Mateusz Klich, 46. 2. Mateusz Klich v Stoke City.
3. 83. 4. 73. 5. 37,004 v Sheffield United.
6. Derby County and West Bromwich Albion.
7. Samuel Sáiz. 8. Queens Park Rangers.
9. Mateusz Klich, Ezgjan Alioski and Kalvin Phillips, 9.
10. Kalvin Phillips and Kiko Casilla. 11. Kiko Casilla.
12. Kemar Roofe, 14.

PAGE 34 · TEAM WORK

Sheffield Wednesday.

Page 36 · A-Z PART TWO

N. Tanguy Ndombele. O. Aston Oxborough.
P. Scott Parker. Q. Domingos Quina
R. Darren Randolph. S. Mo Salah. T. The Tykes.
U. Umbro. V. The Valley. W. Chris Wilder.
X. Granit Xhaka. Y. DeAndre Yedlin. Z. Pablo Zabaleta.

PAGE 44 · HEY REF

1. Direct free kick. 2. Indirect free kick.
3. Yellow card - Caution. 4. Red card - Sending off.
5. Obstruction. 6. Substitution. 7. Offside/foul.
8. Penalty. 9. Offside location. 10. Play on.